table flowers

home decorating workbooks

table flowers

Nikki Tibbles

photography by Simon Brown

RYLAND
PETERS
& SMALL

First published in Great Britain in 1999
by Ryland Peters & Small
Cavendish House
51–55 Mortimer Street
London W1N 7TD

Text copyright © 1999 Nikki Tibbles
Design and photographs copyright
© 1999 Ryland Peters & Small

10 9 8 7 6 5 4 3 2 1

Produced by Sun Fung Offset Binding Co., Ltd
Printed in China

Publishing Director **Anne Ryland**

Head of Design **Gabriella Le Grazie**

Designer **Sally Powell**

Senior Editor **Hilary Mandleberg**

Editorial Assistant **Maddalena Bastianelli**

Production **Rosanna Dickinson**

Illustrator **Lizzie Sanders**

Stylist **Lucy Berridge**

ISBN: 1 84172 004 6

A CIP catalogue record for this book is
available from the British Library.

contents

introduction 6

purest whites 10
rose topiary 12
high-drama hydrangeas 16
tulips in a row 20
contemporary roses 24

moody blues 28
classical anemones 30
romantic table wreath 34
high-profile roses & tulips 38
hydrangea circle 42

glorious oranges 46
tulips in an oak-leaf nest 48
golden delicious 52
fruit & flower urn 56
sunflower burst 60

richest reds 64
romantic roses 66
gothic candelabra 70
mossy anemones 74
roses are red 78

gorgeous greens 82
birch-wrapped parrot tulips 84
limelight roses 88
orient express 92
kitchen-garden cabbages 96

table settings 100
table accessories 102
a few essentials 104
plant directory 108
suppliers & credits 110
acknowledgements 112

IT WAS PURE CHANCE THAT DRAGGED ME INTO THE WORLD OF FLOWERS from a rather unfulfilling career in advertising, but I consider myself so very lucky to have made the change. It all started when a good friend of mine asked me to help her with the flowers for her wedding. I went to look at the venue, gingerly set foot in New Covent Garden Flower Market, and decided upon a theme! I had no idea even of the basics – for instance I didn't know that I was supposed to trim the ends off the flowers before putting them in water! And being so naive, I tackled the whole wedding on my own. It must have been a success though, as nine months later my (still) good friend's sister asked me to do her wedding flowers. The rest, as they say, is history. I gave up my flailing career in advertising and handed back all the trappings of success – the company car, credit cards and so on. I was lucky enough to get a job with a high-street florist where I discovered my hatred of carnations, chrysanthemums and gypsophila. Within six months I had opened my own shop …

Since that time five years ago I have learned so much and, although I have never worked so hard in my life, my love and passion for flowers increases daily. In this book of table flowers I hope to share with you some of my ideas and impart some of the skills I have learned so that you, too, can make arrangements that are unusual, beautiful and full of impact.

Different colours send completely different messages so I decided that the best way to tackle this book was to divide it into colour themes – white, green, red, blue and orange. But before you choose your colour and set about planning your table flowers, there are a few other considerations you should bear in mind.

Firstly look at the space where you will put the flowers. Consider its colour scheme and its scale and proportions. Is it contemporary or traditional? Is the table round or rectangular?

Secondly consider the accessories you have at your disposal. What table linen, dinner service and vases are available? Does the budget run to buying new vases or table linen and a generous quantity of candles and nightlights, or will you have to be content with simply perking up the existing table linen with a richly coloured piece of fabric or some lavish ribbons? Lustrous silks, rustling chiffons and simple muslins may be found in shops and markets everywhere and can be combined with ordinary tablecloths to make something very special, and while it's always nice to lay a table using good linen napkins, it is so much more special to tie them with a beautiful piece of ribbon and have a scented rose or tiny posy of lily of the valley nestling inside.

Especially for a big event, unless money is no object, buy flowers in season and make use of what is in the garden. That way you will be able to afford enough to make an impact. Remember, too, that, although I give lots of ideas for arrangements in this book, you can always adapt them to suit the flowers and foliage that are available.

And finally, think of the mood and atmosphere you want to create. Is it to be coolly stylish and sophisticated, passionate and sexy, or lighthearted and full of fun?

My advice is, to start with, don't try and be too adventurous. Simplicity often brings the best results. And attention to detail is a must too, from the beautifully starched napkin tied with ribbon to the scented candle, the place card or some scattered petals.

I would hope that doing the flowers for a dinner party, wedding, anniversary or simple outdoor lunch is a pleasure, and not another chore, something to add to the already numerous pressures of choosing menus, doing the shopping, deciding what to wear, buying the ubiquitous hat or doing the seating plan. And if you are putting together the flowers for your own party, they should, of course, reflect your personality.

Have fun!

Nikki Tibbles

purest whites

Simple, stylish and contemporary, or utterly traditional – whatever the occasion, wherever the location and no matter what the message, white flowers are always appropriate. Conveying elegance and sophistication, they come in a multitude of shades from bright white through to rich cream, and in enough varieties to take you through all the seasons of the year. You can easily mix them with flowers of any other colour, but that is far too obvious. Dare to be different. Be bold and enjoy the subtle effect that only whites and creams can produce.

left As this display goes to show, an arrangement of flowers does not have to be constrained by a vase. A flower as pure and architectural as the white arum lily, with its beautiful trumpet-shaped flower and its long, elegant stem in contrasting green, looks dazzling simply scattered over a crisp white tabelcloth among white candles and nightlights. For a special-occasion dinner party, you do not have to worry too much about the flowers surviving without water, but in any case, arum lilies will not let you down.

below Floating candles, rose heads and rose petals scattered in a pool of rose-scented water create a mood of mysticism and sensuality. The contrast of the concrete bowl with such romantic flowers as white roses is perhaps a little surprising but adds a slightly primeval note to the occasion. If you don't have a beautiful rough concrete bowl like this one, glass or pale-toned wood will look almost as good.

left Coyly hiding among their broad green leaves, delicately scented dainty white bells of lily of the valley are so charming and pretty and so utterly feminine. Add the finishing touch to an all-white table setting by tying a few stems to each guest's napkin using a bow of white ribbon lightly edged with a touch of contrast stitching.
below You could hardly find a simpler table decoration than this beautifully grained light wood bowl filled with white rose petals.

right Dark green and white make for one of nature's most extreme tonal contrasts – the closest she comes, in fact, to the complete contrast of black and white. Capitalize on nature's work with a larger-than-life table decoration of white hydrangeas and leaves in a pair of striking white rectangular ceramic vases. Too tall for a dinner-party table decoration, this would make an eye-catching centrepiece for a buffet meal or could stand alone at eye level on a tall console table. With their big fluffy flower heads made up of a multitude of tiny florets, hydrangeas are normally thought of as blowsily, eternally romantic, but here the stark white vases and crisply veined deep green leaves create an unexpectedly contemporary graphic effect. Don't be daunted by the fear that vases this tall need flowers on impossibly long stems. Instead, use the old floristry tip of stuffing the vase with crumpled paper or cellophane so the flower heads peep over the edge.

instructions under flap ➤

rose topiary

A mass of white roses makes a traditionally shaped topiary tree into a spectacular centrepiece for a summer wedding party in a marquee or for a formal dinner at home. If you want a more casual look, go for roses in reds and pinks or golds and yellows. Remember to match up your container and pebbles, then add the finishing touches – toning table linen, candles and nightlights, and a scattering of petals all around.

materials & equipment

inner container, 25 cm (10 in) high x 15 cm (6 in) diameter

outer container 28 cm (11 in) high x 18 cm (7 in) diameter

wooden stick, 90 cm (3 ft) long x 2.5 cm (1 in) diameter

sand, to fill

15–20 large pebbles

1 ball floral foam, 15 cm (6 in) diameter

5 cm (2 in) chicken wire, to cover floral foam ball

20 stems berried ivy, 20–30 stems trailing ivy

10 stems snowberry

70 assorted cream and white roses

trowel • quick-drying cement • sheet of paper • paintbrush
white emulsion paint • floristry knife • floristry scissors

7 Trim the snowberries down to 10 cm (4 in).

8 Position the snowberries evenly among the berried ivy and trailing ivy.

9 Trim the roses down to approximately 10 cm (4 in).

10 Push about a third of the roses into the foam ball in groups of three, distributing them evenly among the foliage.

11 Complete the arrangement by adding the remainder of the roses, ensuring that you do not obscure all the foliage and berries. Finally, arrange the colourwashed pebbles around the base of the stick and around the container.

1 Prepare the quick-drying cement according to the manufacturer's instructions, then use it to fill the inner container. Stand the wooden stick in the centre and hold it steady for a few minutes while the cement dries.

2 When the cement has set, place the inner container inside the outer container, then pour sand between the two to keep the inner container stable.

3 Place the pebbles and container on a sheet of paper. Paint the stick and pot white, and give the pebbles a white colourwash. Meanwhile, soak the floral foam ball in water.

4 When the paint has dried, push the soaked floral-foam ball onto the stick. Wrap the chicken wire around the foam ball to keep the foam intact.

5 Trim the lower leaves from the berried ivy, then position the sprigs evenly over the foam ball.

6 Trim the lower leaves from the strands of trailing ivy then position the trimmed strands evenly among the berried ivy.

high-drama hydrangeas

I'm a great fan of masses of one type of flower, whatever the colour, but white is especially beautiful. The full, overblown heads of these hydrangeas make the perfect base for a large-scale arrangement for a special-occasion buffet – perhaps a wedding or christening party. The larger-than-life candles are a must.

materials & equipment

urn, 60 cm (24 in) high x 50 cm (20 in) diameter

plastic sheeting, to fit

5 blocks floral foam, 32 x 23 x 18 cm (13 x 9 x 7in)

30 white hydrangeas

30 stems trailing ivy

florist's tape • floristry scissors • floristry knife • wire cutters • reel wire

5 Divide the ivy into two garlands. Using reel wire, securely attach the end of one garland to one of the handles of the urn. Position the garland around the rim of the urn and secure the other end to the other handle. Repeat on the other side of the urn using the second garland.

6 Trimming their stems to length if necessary, push the first row of hydrangea heads into the foam just above the ivy to form a ring around the urn.

7 To create the highest point of the arrangement, push a single hydrangea head into the middle of the foam, then fill in all the remaining gaps with the rest of the flowers to make an even, domed shape.

1 Line the urn with plastic sheeting, securing the sheeting with florist's tape. Meanwhile, thoroughly soak the blocks of floral foam in a bucket of water.

2 Fill the urn with the foam, cutting it to fit using a sharp knife. The foam should protrude over the top of the urn by about 7 cm (3 in) to enable you to give the arrangement a domed effect. If necessary, stand the blocks on top of the foam offcuts.

3 Use more tape to secure the foam to the edge of the urn.

4 Strip all the lower leaves from the hydrangeas, leaving just a few as a collar around each flower head.

tulips in a row

This table arrangement couldn't be easier to achieve. It's just three
simple glass tank vases filled with vermiculite and tulips, all lined
up in a row. Use as many vases as the length of your table allows,
but for best effect, three is the minimum. Finish off with a collar
of ivy leaves around the base of the tulips, plus a few more
leaves pinned to the tablecloth. Buy flowers in season
for minimum expense and maximum impact.

materials & equipment

3 cylindrical containers, 18 cm (7 in) high x 7 cm (3 in) diameter

3 glass tank vases, 15 x 15 x 20 cm (6 x 6 x 8 in)

vermiculite, to fill

60 white tulips

approximately 20 large ivy leaves

floristry scissors • raffia • dressmaker's pins

5 Place each bunch in its own vase. They must fit snugly for stability. Top up each square vase with more vermiculite to conceal the top of the inner container.

6 Push three or four ivy leaves around the base of the tulips in each of the vases.

7 Arrange the three vases in a line on the table, adding the finishing touch by pinning ivy leaves to the tablecloth.

1 Place a cylindrical container in the centre of each of the glass tank vases. Pour in vermiculite to fill the space between each vase and its cylinder.

2 Pour in water to half fill each cylindrical container.

3 Using sharp scissors, trim the tulips to 30 cm (12 in).

4 Divide the tulips into three equal bunches and secure with raffia near the base of the stems.

contemporary roses

Concrete is so contemporary and I love juxtaposing it with roses – that most traditional of flowers. Here the cream and white flowers echo the colour of the concrete, but their soft roundness makes a great textural contrast. Weaving lengths of trailing ivy through the roses gives volume, while square white candles add clean lines.

materials & equipment

concrete bowl, 32 cm (13 in) high x 28 cm (11 in) diameter

plastic sheeting, to fit

3 blocks floral foam, 32 x 23 x 18 cm (13 x 9 x 7 in)

12 stems trailing ivy

20 stems berried ivy

20 sprigs rosemary

90 cream and white roses

floristry scissors • florist's tape • floristry knife

6 Using scissors or a knife, trim the roses down to approximately 18 cm (7 in), then strip the lower leaves from the stems and remove all the thorns.

7 Grouping the roses in clusters of three of the same variety, distribute them evenly in the floral foam to create a gently rounded dome shape.

8 Finally, remove the leaves from the ends of the remaining trailing ivy, cut their tips off, remove the leaves from the tips, then poke both ends in among the roses to form graceful loops of foliage over the dome of flowers and foliage.

26

1 Cut a piece of plastic sheeting to size and use it to line the concrete bowl, taping it to the bowl with florist's tape. Meanwhile, soak the blocks of floral foam in a bucket of water.

2 Fill the bowl with the soaked floral foam, shaping it to fit with a sharp knife and standing it on the offcuts so it comes about 5 cm (2 in) above the top of the bowl.

3 Tape the foam in place, then loosely twist together three or four of the strands of trailing ivy and position them around the rim of the bowl. Attach the ivy with more tape.

4 Trim the berried ivy and rosemary down to about 7 cm (3 in) then remove the lower leaves.

5 Push the ivy and rosemary into the foam, distributing it evenly all over.

left A mass of delphiniums in a big silver vase makes a dramatic statement – impossible to ignore and utterly reminiscent of summer. This arrangement would make an amazing display on a summer buffet table, with a pool of toning fabric at its feet. The simple touch of encircling the flowers with lengths of trailing ivy lifts the arrangement out of the ordinary, while the silver vase makes it truly contemporary.

right Silver again. Tiny flowers peeping over the top edge of a large vase make an unusual combination. I love the proportions of this arrangement and the bold effect of the lilac and silver together.

below Nothing could be simpler than this arrangement. Just line up a row of blue glass bottles and add a stem of deep blue delphiniums to each. Use any bottles, as long as they match one another, and as long as the flowers match them, too.

moody blues

Cool and refreshing or richly moody, blues, lilacs, violets and purples make up one of the most expressive colour ranges. They can hint at the vastness of sea and sky or can draw you in to an enclosed world of deep dark emotion. In flower arranging it's amazing how all these shades work well together and I love them for their versatility. At a formal dinner they can be grown up and sophisticated, while for a simple lunch in the garden with friends, they become calmly unassuming.

right Sinuously tall, these three vases normally hold single lily specimens, but here they have been commandeered for delphiniums and the water has been dyed blue with food colouring. The effect is simple yet striking, and very inexpensive. You could try other combinations too – orange water with marigolds, red with red anemones, and so on.

far right What brings together an eccentric mix of vases so they look just made for each other? The answer – fill them with just one type of flower, in this case round lush heads of blue hydrangeas. The chunkiness of the flowers complements the vases perfectly.

classical anemones

For table, substitute floor. Throw over a heavy linen cloth, add some plump cushions, slate 'placemats', lavishly be-ribboned napkins, rich blue candle holders, a scattering of irises and an oversized centrepiece consisting of a large iron urn filled with open-faced blue anemones encircled with ivy. The result – wildly romantic, yet wholly up to date and laid back. Invite your best friends over and enjoy!

materials & equipment

urn, 38 cm (15 in) high x 43 cm (17 in) diameter

plastic sheeting, to fit

plastic bowl, 15 cm (6 in) high x 37 cm (15 in) diameter

1.5 cm (½ in) chicken wire, to fit the mouth of the urn

80–100 blue anemones

7–10 stems trailing ivy

floristry scissors • florist's tape • wire cutters

6 Working outwards in a spiral, arrange the rest of the anemones to form a slightly flattened dome shape. As you approach the edges, trim the anemone stems down further as required to maintain the correct shape.

7 Loosely twine the trailing strands of ivy around the neck of the urn, holding them in place with pieces of florist's tape concealed among the foliage.

1 Use scissors to cut a piece of plastic sheeting to size and line the urn with it, holding it in place around the urn with florist's tape.

2 Place the plastic bowl inside the lined urn and fill it two-thirds full of water.

3 Using wire cutters, cut the chicken wire to fit across the mouth of the urn and hold it in place with more florist's tape.

4 Trim the stems of the anemones down to 25 cm (10 in).

5 Start by positioning a cluster of three or four anemones in the centre of the urn to make the highest point of the arrangement.

romantic table wreath

This is the most traditional arrangement in the book, but the mass of candles brings it bang up to date. The trick for a display like this one is to work with flowers of similar shape and to keep the foliage types to a minimum. The grape hyacinths wrapped in velvet ribbon add an extra layer of interest.

materials & equipment

3 candles, 18 cm (7 in) high x 7 cm (3 in) diameter

1 plastic-based floral foam ring, 37 cm (15 in) diameter

20–30 stems berried ivy

12 lilac roses

10–15 blue lisianthus

50 blue anemones

60 blue grape hyacinths

1 m (1¼ yd) blue velvet ribbon x 1.5 cm (½ in) wide

medium-gauge stub wires • floristry scissors • florist's tape
floristry knife • dressmaker's pins

5 Trim the lisianthus and anemones to 10 cm (4 in) and push them into the foam, a cluster of each between each candle.

6 Make six bunches of grape hyacinths and wrap them in velvet ribbon, pinning the ribbon to fasten it securely.

7 Lay two bunches between each candle, positioning them so the stems of one bunch face inwards, and the stems of the other face outwards.

1 Bend three medium-gauge stub wires into hairpin shapes and use florist's tape to attach them around the base of each of three candles, leaving about 4 cm (1½ in) of wire protruding. Meanwhile, soak the floral foam ring.

2 Push the candles into the foam ring.

3 Trim the berried ivy to 10 cm (4 in) and push it into the foam ring, spacing it evenly around and between the candles

4 Trim the roses to 10 cm (4 in) and push them into the foam ring in groups of four in front of each candle.

high-profile roses & tulips

I love the unexpected, especially if it doesn't look or feel contrived.
A tall cylindrical vase like this, begging to take centre stage, would
usually be filled with tall flowers. Instead I have made a dome
of lilac tulips and roses. Silver and lilac work so well together.
For once, the flowers play a supporting role.

materials & equipment

metal vase, 65 cm (26 in) high x 25 cm (10 in) diameter

cellophane or plastic sheeting, to fill

40 lilac roses

40 lilac tulips

7 stems trailing ivy

floristry scissors • floristry knife • raffia • wire cutters
reel wire • florist's tape

5 Continue adding roses and tulips, four or five at a time, still placing them over the bunch at an angle to maintain the shape.

6 Finish by securing the raffia in a double knot. The stems should go in a spiral direction and the finished bunch should be quite solid. Trim the stems.

7 Twist the trailing strands of ivy together, holding them at intervals with reel wire to form a circle.

8 Add water to the vase then position the circle of ivy around the top like a collar, holding it in place with several small pieces of florist's tape. Finish by positioning the tied bunch of tulips and roses in the vase.

1 Pack the lower two-thirds of the vase with crumpled cellophane or plastic sheeting to form a support for the flowers.

2 Use scissors to trim the stems of the roses and tulips down to about 25 cm (10 in). Remove any thorns from the roses and all the foliage from the lower part of the stems.

3 Hold a few roses and tulips in one hand, crossing the stems over one another so the flower heads fan out slightly. Tie tightly with raffia about one-third of the way down, leaving a long end of raffia.

4 Turn the bunch slightly in your hand, then add a few more stems of roses and tulips, crossing these over so they also fan out and tying them into the bunch with the long end of raffia in the same way.

hydrangea circle

Using design foam board means that you can cut your table centrepiece to any shape you want. I have chosen a circle, but you can let your imagination run wild with a freeform shape. Fill it with masses of large-headed flowers. These hydrangeas are perfect, but sunflowers or gerberas would also look great. Roses make a dazzling choice too. Finish off with as many candles as you can possibly muster.

materials & equipment

1 piece design foam board, 60 x 60 cm (24 x 24 in)

5 candles, 15 cm (6 in) high x 6 cm (2¹/₂ in) diameter

30 large ivy leaves

30–40 blue hydrangeas

nail • string • pencil • floristry knife • florist's tape • 20 matchsticks
dressmaker's pins • floristry scissors

glorious oranges

In past ages orange evoked victory, success and wealth, and in the eighteenth century only brides from affluent families were permitted to wear orange flowers. Now that symbolism plays less part in our lives, we associate oranges and yellows with warmth, friendliness and happiness. They conjure up a setting sun, exotic spices from distant lands or the first days of autumn as the leaves start to change colour.

above left When I first visited India my senses were assaulted and the memory I have of women and children sitting on the steps of temples among mountains of marigold heads is as vivid now as it was then. This garland of marigold heads strung on wire is my homage to a glorious country. *far left* Fill a row of simple galvanized vases with floral foam, push the poppies in with a collar of ivy leaves and just watch them as their hairy stems bend and curl. *left* A single rich orange poppy tucked into a gold napkin ring has something of the Midas touch.

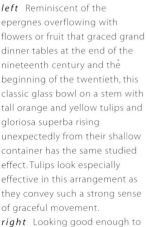

left Reminiscent of the epergnes overflowing with flowers or fruit that graced grand dinner tables at the end of the nineteenth century and the beginning of the twentieth, this classic glass bowl on a stem with tall orange and yellow tulips and gloriosa superba rising unexpectedly from their shallow container has the same studied effect. Tulips look especially effective in this arrangement as they convey such a strong sense of graceful movement.
right Looking good enough to eat, a bamboo skewer threaded with marigold heads and rose petals makes an unusual side order for a dinner party. Other flowers that work well with this treatment include anemones, orchid florets and rose buds.

instructions under flap ➤

tulips in an oak-leaf nest

Orange and yellow tulips conjure up the spirit of spring but now they are available at almost any time of year. Mix them with autumnal leaves for a beautiful blend of the seasons. The arrangement stands on bronze chiffon on top of a white cloth. Pomegranates make a display that looks good enough to eat.

materials & equipment

glass bowl, 25 cm (10 in) high x 30 cm (12 in) diameter

glass bowl, 23 cm (9 in) high x 23 cm (9 in) diameter

oak leaves, to fill

35 yellow tulips

35 orange tulips

floristry knife • raffia • floristry scissors

6 Use scissors to trim the hydrangea stems down to about 7 cm (3 in), then remove any foliage.

7 Starting at the edge of the foam board, push the hydrangea heads into the foam to make a circle of flowers that overlaps the ivy leaves slightly.

8 Continue placing the hydrangea heads so they butt up around the candles. Fill the foam circle with more hydrangea heads to conceal any gaps.

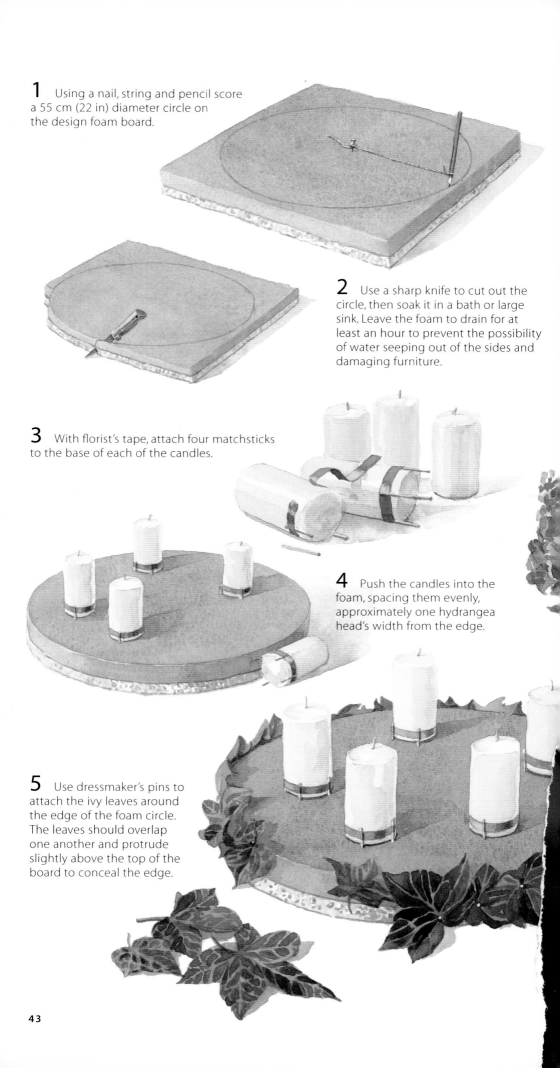

1 Using a nail, string and pencil score a 55 cm (22 in) diameter circle on the design foam board.

2 Use a sharp knife to cut out the circle, then soak it in a bath or large sink. Leave the foam to drain for at least an hour to prevent the possibility of water seeping out of the sides and damaging furniture.

3 With florist's tape, attach four matchsticks to the base of each of the candles.

4 Push the candles into the foam, spacing them evenly, approximately one hydrangea head's width from the edge.

5 Use dressmaker's pins to attach the ivy leaves around the edge of the foam circle. The leaves should overlap one another and protrude slightly above the top of the board to conceal the edge.

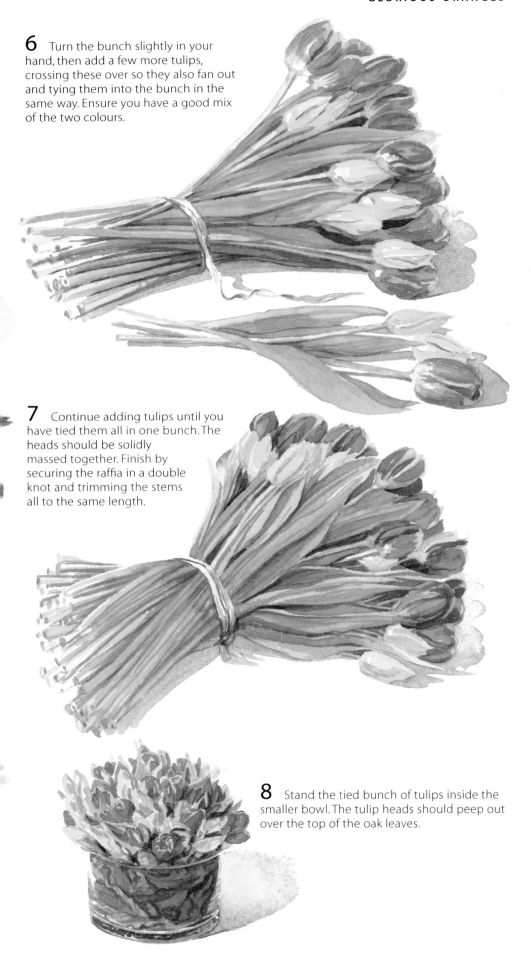

6 Turn the bunch slightly in your hand, then add a few more tulips, crossing these over so they also fan out and tying them into the bunch in the same way. Ensure you have a good mix of the two colours.

7 Continue adding tulips until you have tied them all in one bunch. The heads should be solidly massed together. Finish by securing the raffia in a double knot and trimming the stems all to the same length.

8 Stand the tied bunch of tulips inside the smaller bowl. The tulip heads should peep out over the top of the oak leaves.

1 Stand the smaller bowl inside the larger one and fill the smaller bowl two-thirds full of water.

2 Use a generous amount of oak leaves to fill the space between the two bowls.

3 Use a knife to cut the tulips down to 30 cm (12 in) and remove the foliage from the lower part of the stems.

4 Hold a few tulips – some of each colour – in one hand, crossing the stems over one another so the flower heads fan out slightly.

5 Tie tightly with raffia about two-thirds of the way down, leaving a long end of raffia.

golden delicious

A long, low arrangement like this one makes an ideal centrepiece
for a rectangular table. Remember not·to make the arrangement
too tall, or your guests will be talking to the flowers all evening
which is not ideal! Here I painted a galvanized container gold
to work with the golden tones of this collection of roses,
arum lilies and gloriosa superba, but any colour is
possible, depending on your colour scheme.

materials & equipment

galvanized trough, 60 x 12 x 10 cm (24 x 5 x 4 in)

8 blocks floral foam, 8 x 11 x 8 cm (3¹/₄ x 4¹/₂ x 3¹/₄ in)

plastic sheeting, to fit

3 candles, 22 cm (9 in) high x 10 cm (4 in) diameter

12–15 sprigs ivy

18 yellow roses, shaded red, 10 yellow roses, 33 terracotta roses, 27 orange roses

9 mango-coloured arum lilies

24 gloriosa superba

12 stems trailing ivy

gold paint • paintbrush • floristry scissors • florist's tape • floristry knife
medium-gauge stub wires

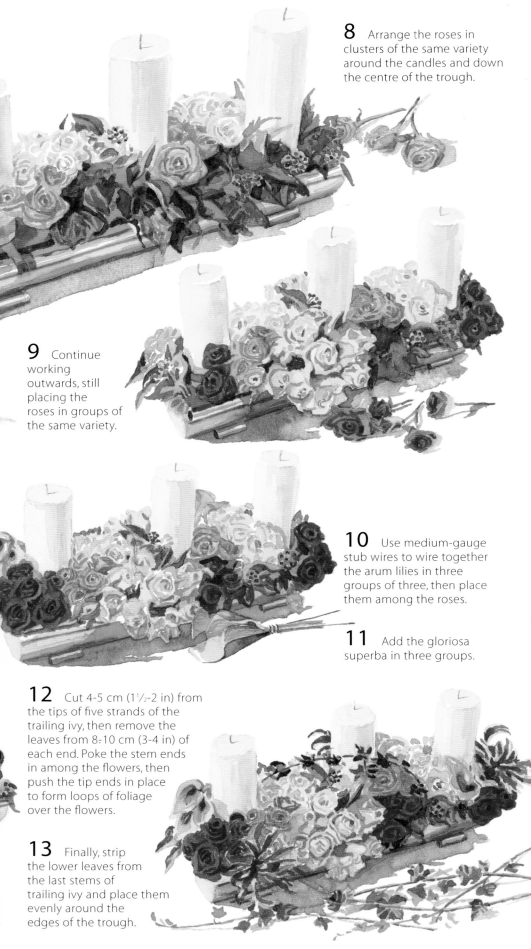

8 Arrange the roses in clusters of the same variety around the candles and down the centre of the trough.

9 Continue working outwards, still placing the roses in groups of the same variety.

10 Use medium-gauge stub wires to wire together the arum lilies in three groups of three, then place them among the roses.

11 Add the gloriosa superba in three groups.

12 Cut 4-5 cm (1½-2 in) from the tips of five strands of the trailing ivy, then remove the leaves from 8÷10 cm (3-4 in) of each end. Poke the stem ends in among the flowers, then push the tip ends in place to form loops of foliage over the flowers.

13 Finally, strip the lower leaves from the last stems of trailing ivy and place them evenly around the edges of the trough.

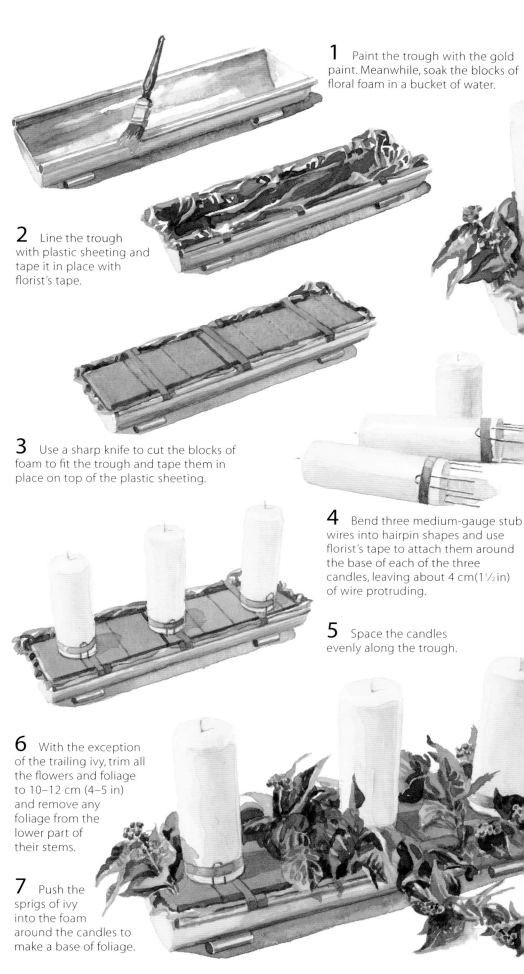

1 Paint the trough with the gold paint. Meanwhile, soak the blocks of floral foam in a bucket of water.

2 Line the trough with plastic sheeting and tape it in place with florist's tape.

3 Use a sharp knife to cut the blocks of foam to fit the trough and tape them in place on top of the plastic sheeting.

4 Bend three medium-gauge stub wires into hairpin shapes and use florist's tape to attach them around the base of each of the three candles, leaving about 4 cm(1½ in) of wire protruding.

5 Space the candles evenly along the trough.

6 With the exception of the trailing ivy, trim all the flowers and foliage to 10–12 cm (4–5 in) and remove any foliage from the lower part of their stems.

7 Push the sprigs of ivy into the foam around the candles to make a base of foliage.

fruit & flower urn

I don't often use fruits and flowers together but with this
container it would be a pity not to. Glossy satsumas with their
leaves still attached look great, or you could use kumquats, lemons
or limes if you wish. When you add the flowers, keep them in
groups of the same type. The effect will be more dramatic. Filling
the stem of the wire urn with lichen is a nice touch. It helps
to balance out the weight of the fruit and flowers above.

materials & equipment

wire urn, 45 cm (18 in) high x 25 cm (10 in) diameter

lichen, to fill

2 blocks floral foam, 23 x 11 x 8 cm (9 x 4¹/₂ x 3¹/₄ in)

plastic bowl, 12 cm (5 in) high x 20 cm (8 in) diameter

15–20 stems berried ivy

8 satsumas

3 stems hypericum berries

3 orange tulips, 6 yellow tulips

3 orange poppies

10 orange roses, 9 terracotta roses, 8 yellow roses, 8 yellow roses, shaded red

floristry knife • florist's tape • heavy-gauge stub wires

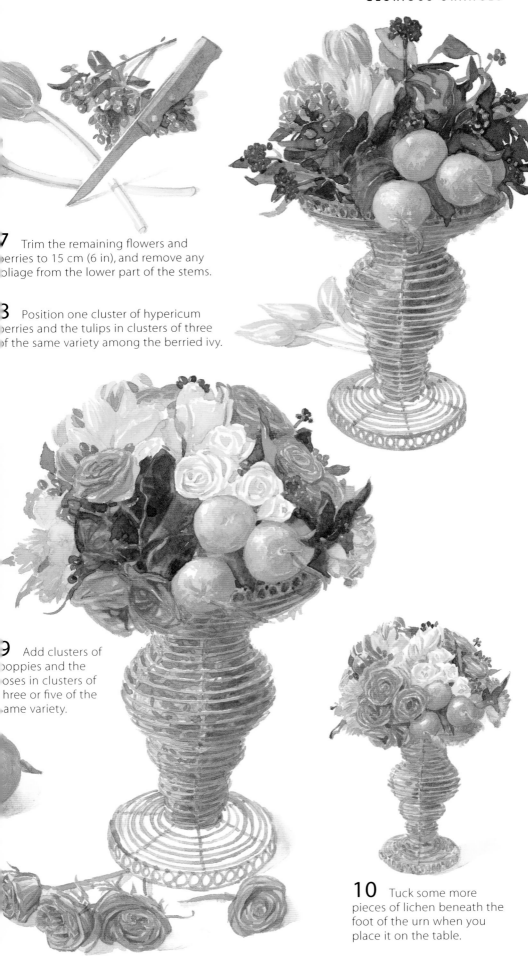

7 Trim the remaining flowers and berries to 15 cm (6 in), and remove any foliage from the lower part of the stems.

8 Position one cluster of hypericum berries and the tulips in clusters of three of the same variety among the berried ivy.

9 Add clusters of poppies and the roses in clusters of three or five of the same variety.

10 Tuck some more pieces of lichen beneath the foot of the urn when you place it on the table.

1 Fill the wire urn about two-thirds full with lichen, pushing it carefully down so there are no gaps. Meanwhile, soak the blocks of floral foam in water.

2 Use a sharp knife to trim the soaked floral foam to fit the plastic bowl. Stand it on the offcuts so it comes approximately 2.5 cm (1 in) above the edge of the bowl. Place the foam in the plastic bowl and hold it in place with florist's tape.

3 Insert the bowl on top of the lichen in the wire urn and fill the space between the bowl and the urn with some more lichen.

4 Trim the berried ivy down to about 15 cm (6 in), remove the foliage from the lower part of the stems, then position it in the floral foam to give the basic rounded shape of the arrangement.

5 Use two heavy-gauge stub wires to wire up each of the satsumas.

6 Position the satsumas in two loose clusters of four around the edge of the floral foam.

sunflower burst

Sunny yellow sunflowers bring a smile to most faces and dressing them in a birch-twig skirt might even elicit a chuckle. This simple idea based on a dome of sunflowers in a tall vase produces stylishly dramatic results – even more so when the twig skirt overlaps the edge of the table. What can you think of that would be more fun as the centrepiece for an informal late-summer or autumn drinks party?

materials & equipment

25 birch twigs

glass vase, 90 cm (36 in) high x 30 cm (12 in) diameter

5 stems trailing ivy

20 sunflowers

floristry knife • wire cutters • reel wire • raffia • floristry scissors

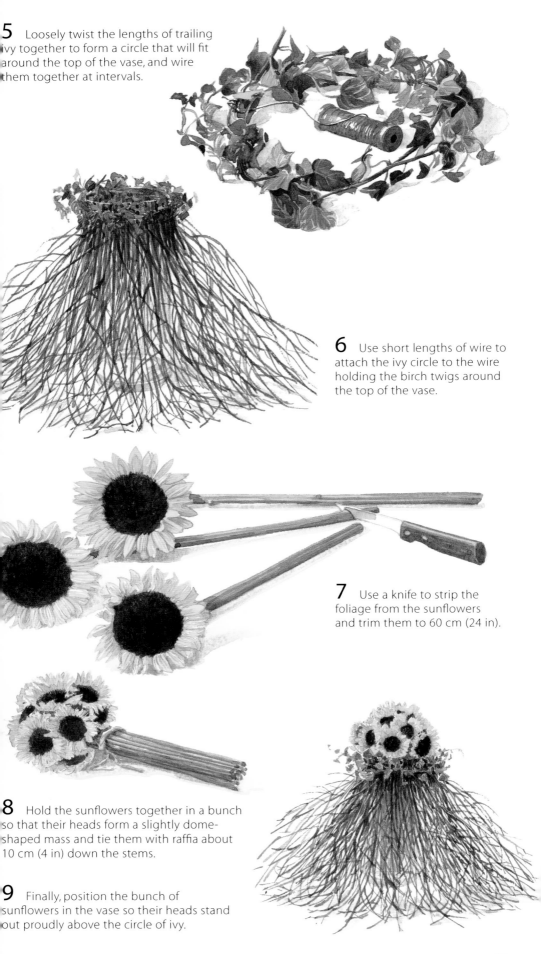

5 Loosely twist the lengths of trailing ivy together to form a circle that will fit around the top of the vase, and wire them together at intervals.

6 Use short lengths of wire to attach the ivy circle to the wire holding the birch twigs around the top of the vase.

7 Use a knife to strip the foliage from the sunflowers and trim them to 60 cm (24 in).

8 Hold the sunflowers together in a bunch so that their heads form a slightly dome-shaped mass and tie them with raffia about 10 cm (4 in) down the stems.

9 Finally, position the bunch of sunflowers in the vase so their heads stand out proudly above the circle of ivy.

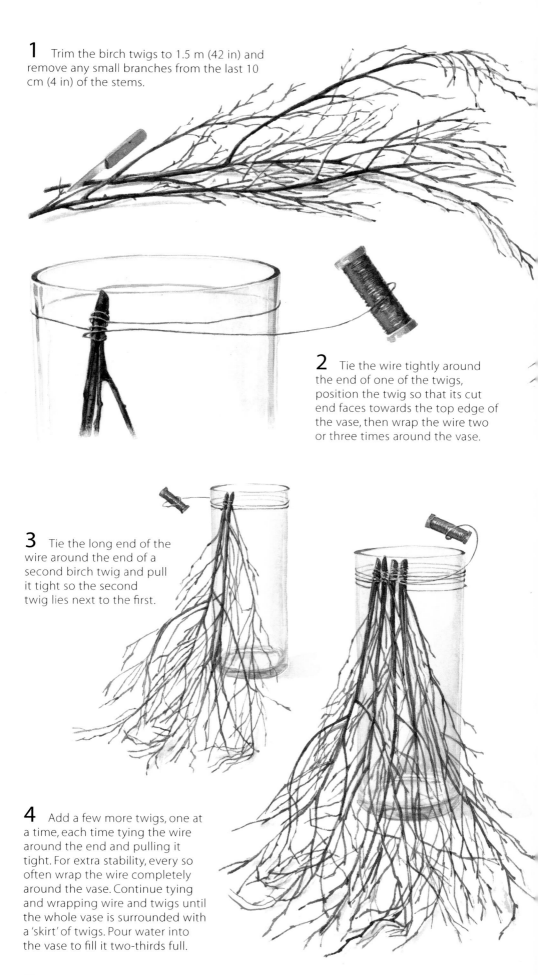

1 Trim the birch twigs to 1.5 m (42 in) and remove any small branches from the last 10 cm (4 in) of the stems.

2 Tie the wire tightly around the end of one of the twigs, position the twig so that its cut end faces towards the top edge of the vase, then wrap the wire two or three times around the vase.

3 Tie the long end of the wire around the end of a second birch twig and pull it tight so the second twig lies next to the first.

4 Add a few more twigs, one at a time, each time tying the wire around the end and pulling it tight. For extra stability, every so often wrap the wire completely around the vase. Continue tying and wrapping wire and twigs until the whole vase is surrounded with a 'skirt' of twigs. Pour water into the vase to fill it two-thirds full.

right If you thought goldfish bowls were strictly for fish, then think again. Here three velvety red gerberas have each taken up residence in a goldfish bowl. Out goes the fish food, in goes some red-tinted water.
below The compact heads, rich colour and unbelievable texture of armfuls of roses are perfect when it comes to making arrangements where a specific shape is required, as in this wondrous cross.

richest reds

Red is the most sexy of colours. It says more than any other colour about how brave you are. It will set the scene for a dreamy, tender rendezvous or for passionate, seductive encounters, for festive mulled wine parties with friends, or for intimate dinners for two. Cast a spell with a table covering of deep red silk chiffon, light a mass of scented candles and a blazing log fire, then sit back and enjoy the magic. Many flowers come in red, but the rose is the most romantic of them all, in every tone from pale delicate shell pink to the deepest darkest richest reds and burgundies. Use them *en masse*, their tones blending in glorious textural effect. You've got nothing to lose. Go for it!

left Fill a rectangular glass vase with rose petals in shades of pink and red, and lay a red-chiffon-tied bunch of deep red, almost black, arum lilies among them. The delicately scented sexily elegant arum lilies make a decadent, highly indulgent combination with the rose petals and will survive without water for a few hours for a special occasion. You could try for a similar effect using white rose petals with white lilies or yellow and apricot petals with mango-coloured arums. Two or three stems of sculptural gloriosa superba, phalaenopsis orchids, eucharis lilies or of papyrus, or a cluster of sweet peas or tulips would also look the part.

left I love the unexpected and what could be more unexpected than this bunch of tulips plunged upside down in a clear glass vase? Notice how I have used half-open tulips with just enough colour peeping tantalizingly out to harmonize with the ribbon tie, and how I have chosen a vase that echoes the shape of the flowers so they fit snugly inside in perfect harmony. If you have a wide-mouthed bowl you might like to try the same effect with a bunch of hydrangeas, peonies, sunflowers or luxurious, open-headed roses, while a tall rectangular vase would look great with narcissi, arum lilies or tuberoses.

below For me, peonies with their fat, blowsy heads, are the epitome of summer and romance. With their silken sheeny reds, bubble-gum pinks and seashell creams and ivories, they are my very favourite flower. Normally thought of as a flower for traditionalists, it's quite a surprise to see three bunches of them massed in matching galvanized buckets. Suddenly they look crisp and surprisingly contemporary. A few stems of berried ivy threaded among them prevents them from being over-saccharine. Galvanized pots in different sizes are great for giving a new lease of life to other traditional summer flowers, too. You could try a mass of lavender, sweet peas, delphiniums, dahlias, alliums, foxtail lilies or poppies. The trick is, don't mix them.

romantic roses

After a long, indulgent bath scented with rose bath oil, throw layers
of pink silk chiffon on the table, top with globes of deep red roses,
light your favourite candles and enjoy an intimate dinner for two.
This table decoration cries out for a sexy meal of oysters, asparagus
and chocolate, plus copious amounts of the best champagne.
If it's total self-indulgence you're after, you could even ask
your local florist to supply the flowers – just this once.

materials & equipment

3 balls floral foam, 18 cm (7 in) diameter

3 shallow dishes, to hold floral foam balls

150–180 deep red roses

deep red rose petals, for scattering

florist's tape • floristry scissors

4 Work outwards in a spiral towards the base of each ball, pushing the roses into the foam to cover it. Stand back from the arrangements from time to time to make sure you are working evenly. If necessary, trim the roses further to achieve the correct shape.

5 Hide the edges of the dish with the last roses positioned almost horizontally. Push a few of the reserved rose leaves in among the flowers.

6 Arrange the three rose balls on the table and decorate the cloth with a scattering of matching rose petals.

1 Soak the three floral foam balls in a bucket of water, then tape each one onto a shallow round dish using florist's tape.

2 Use scissors to trim the roses to approximately 2.5 cm (1 in) and remove the foliage from the lower part of the stems. Set aside a few leaves to use later.

3 Position the first roses at the centre of each ball.

gothic candelabra

If high drama is what you want, then this is a certain way of achieving it. No-one could miss an enormous candelabra like this one in the centre of a buffet table. An object with so much attitude needs attention-seeking colours and accessories to go with it – deep red and pink flowers, wintry berries and lichen-covered branches, a rich-coloured damask cloth, burgundy wine glasses, piles of apples and yet more candles.

materials & equipment

2-tier candelabra, 1.8 m (6 ft) high

10–15 stems trailing ivy

1 floral foam ring, 40 cm (16 in) diameter, 1 floral foam ring, 34 cm (14 in) diameter

20 stems rosemary

4–5 lichen-covered larch branches

· 15 red-green hydrangeas

15 stems spiraea

20 deep red roses, 20 pink roses, 10 red spray roses

30 mauve anemones

red Parrot tulips

7 candles, 45 cm (18 in) high x 4 cm (1½ in) diameter

apples, candles and ivy leaves, for decoration

medium-gauge stub wires • floristry scissors
florist's tape • floristry knife • dressmaker's pins

5 Trim the hydrangeas down to 20 cm (8 in) remove their lower leaves and distribute them evenly among the foliage together with the spiraea, trimmed to the same length.

6 Trim the roses down to 20 cm (8 in), then position them in clusters of three or five of the same variety.

7 Add clusters of the anemones and Parrot tulips together with the stems of spray roses, all trimmed to about 20 cm (8 in).

8 Finally, position the candles in the candelabra and decorate the table around the base of the candelabra with apples, candles and ivy leaves pinned to the tablecloth.

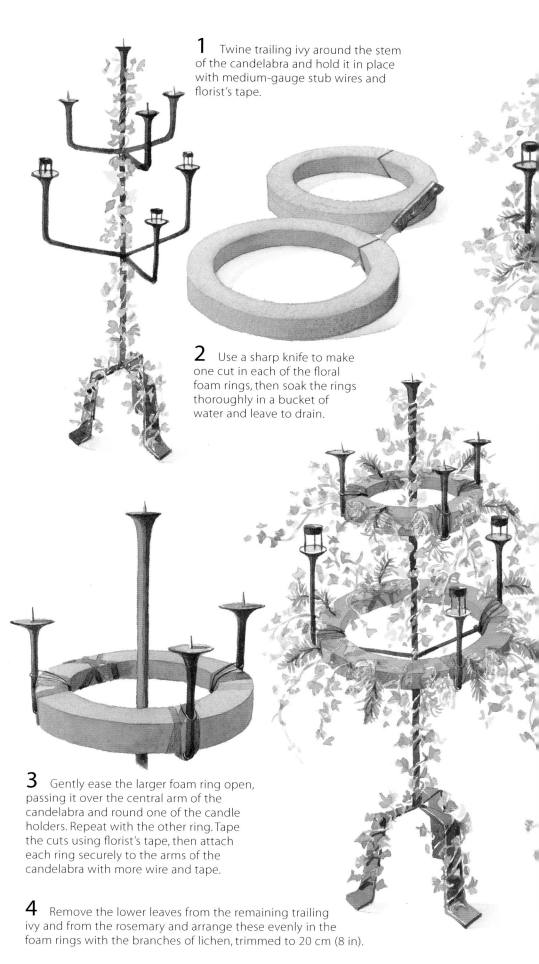

1 Twine trailing ivy around the stem of the candelabra and hold it in place with medium-gauge stub wires and florist's tape.

2 Use a sharp knife to make one cut in each of the floral foam rings, then soak the rings thoroughly in a bucket of water and leave to drain.

3 Gently ease the larger foam ring open, passing it over the central arm of the candelabra and round one of the candle holders. Repeat with the other ring. Tape the cuts using florist's tape, then attach each ring securely to the arms of the candelabra with more wire and tape.

4 Remove the lower leaves from the remaining trailing ivy and from the rosemary and arrange these evenly in the foam rings with the branches of lichen, trimmed to 20 cm (8 in).

mossy anemones

I feel really at home with simple arrangements like this one.
A mass of one type of flower in a plain glass tank vase lined with
moss makes an ideal table centrepiece or could be used anywhere
in the house. If you want a more contemporary look, substitute
a galvanized pot and omit the moss. Line up a row of deep
red square candles and serve with fiery orange glasses
for the ultimate fizzing table decoration.

materials & equipment

glass tank vase, 20 x 20 x 25 cm (8 x 8 x 10 in)

glass tank vase, 15 x 15 x 20 cm (6 x 6 x 8 in)

5 cm (2 in) chicken wire, to fill smaller vase

bun or sphagnum moss, to fill

50 red anemones

5 stems trailing ivy

floristry scissors • florist's tape • wire cutters • reel wire

6 Continue placing the anemones, working outwards in a spiral towards the edge of the inner vase and trimming their stems further if necessary to achieve a pleasing shape.

7 Twist the trailing strands of ivy together, holding them at intervals with reel wire.

8 Complete the arrangement by positioning the ivy in a circle around the top of the glass vase so that it conceals the inner container from view. Hold the ivy in place with florist's tape.

1 Fill the smaller vase with the crumpled chicken wire held in place with florist's tape. Put the smaller vase inside the larger one.

2 Fill the space between the two vases with the moss.

3 Add water to the inner vase, filling it two-thirds full.

4 Use scissors to trim the anemones down to about 20 cm (8 in).

5 Position the first stems in the centre of the wire-filled inner vase.

roses are red

Roses have to be my favourite flower and what better way to use them than *en masse* in a stemmed glass bowl – the modern-day equivalent of an old-fashioned rose bowl. They make the perfect accompaniment to a special-occasion afternoon tea. Go completely over the top with a pink tablecloth, napkins tied with rose-embroidered ribbon, stripey pink and white china and masses of scattered rose petals. Tiny pink-iced cakes are a must.

materials & equipment

glass bowl with a stem, 40 cm (16 in) high x 30 cm (12 in) diameter

8–10 stems trailing ivy

100 assorted red and dark red roses

floristry scissors • florist's tape • wire cutters • reel wire

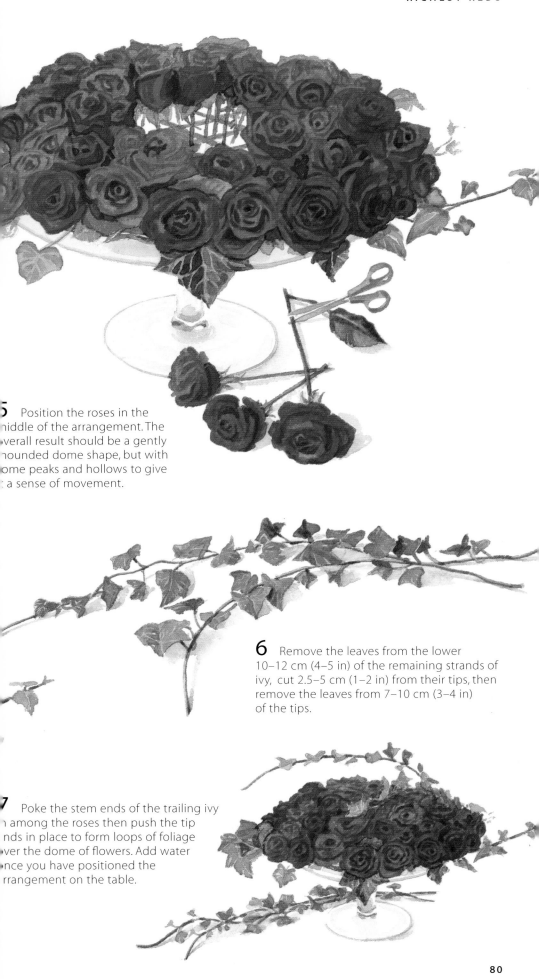

5 Position the roses in the middle of the arrangement. The overall result should be a gently rounded dome shape, but with some peaks and hollows to give a sense of movement.

6 Remove the leaves from the lower 10–12 cm (4–5 in) of the remaining strands of ivy, cut 2.5–5 cm (1–2 in) from their tips, then remove the leaves from 7–10 cm (3–4 in) of the tips.

7 Poke the stem ends of the trailing ivy among the roses then push the tip ends in place to form loops of foliage over the dome of flowers. Add water once you have positioned the arrangement on the table.

1 Make a grid of florist's tape across the mouth of the glass bowl and finish it with a circle of tape around the top of the bowl.

2 Twist two or three trailing strands of ivy together, holding them at intervals with reel wire to form a circle.

3 Place the ivy circle around the top of the bowl and hold it in place with small pieces of florist's tape.

4 Cutting the roses to length as you proceed, arrange them in blocks of the same variety, working from the outer edge of the bowl towards the centre. The roses around the edge of the bowl should have shorter stems than those closer to the centre.

gorgeous greens

Nature gives us so many different tones and shades of green and so many textures, that it's hard to know where to start. Green flowers or bamboo create a modern, almost minimalist feel, yet trugs of ornamental cabbages are very 'country'. The choice is yours. And green is possibly the easiest of all the colours to use to produce a grand, massed effect. Try armfuls of beech or birch foliage or glorious hosta leaves in large cylindrical glass vases or galvanized buckets. And if you can rob them from your garden, they cost nothing at all. Things don't get much better than that.

above left Raid your greengrocer's shop to make an arrangement that proves that it's quantity that matters, not quality. Here I've simply taken a mass of reddish-green curly kale and stuffed it into a plain glass bowl. Other humble green vegetables would do the trick too. Why not try cabbage, spinach or some of those frilly-leafed lettuce leaves?

above right Mind-your-own business plants have a great textural quality and come in several different greens. Make the most of their differences and similarities by lining them up on the table with a defining edge of bright green bamboo canes.

left Asparagus fern is normally considered to be nothing more than an inexpensive filler, but pack it into a large cylindrical glass vase and wow! See how amazingly wild and untamed it suddenly looks.

right and below Arum lilies and
orchids are two of the most
architectural flowers you could
hope to find and in shades of
green they have an almost other-
worldly look. Here they stand layer
upon layer, the tightly bound arum
lilies on top surrounded by orchid
florets, and the vase beneath
packed with yet more orchids. Tiny
flashes of contrasting red in the
throats and on the petals of the
orchids look as if they have been
painted on for special effect.

left There are a few occasions
when the constraints of making
an arrangement to stand on a
table become too great, and this
is one of them. Starting with a
starkly minimalist room setting
and a celadon-green glazed
Japanese tea set, I immediately
had an image of this Zen-like,
flower-free installation. And where
else to put it but on the floor? All
it takes is nine stems of papyrus,
three blocks of floral foam, three
enormously chunky stems of dark
green bamboo and a clutch of
cream and green-toned bamboo-
like candles. But what an
impression it makes! You just feel
like kneeling in front of it to
meditate on the simple things of
life and drink jasmine tea. And on
the grounds that in Japan the
floor sometimes serves as a table,
perhaps I can be forgiven for
including this arrangement here.

birch-wrapped parrot tulips

Lime-green Parrot tulips and variegated hosta leaves make an irresistible combination. Wrap the bowl with birch twigs for added texture. Tulips work well with any shape of vase, so let the shape of the table be your guide – a round vase for a round table, a square one for a square or rectangular table. Easy!

materials & equipment

glass bowl, 23 cm (9 in) high x 25 cm (10 in) diameter

6 birch twigs

50 green and white Parrot tulips

30 variegated hosta leaves

wire cutters • reel wire • floristry knife • floristry scissors • raffia

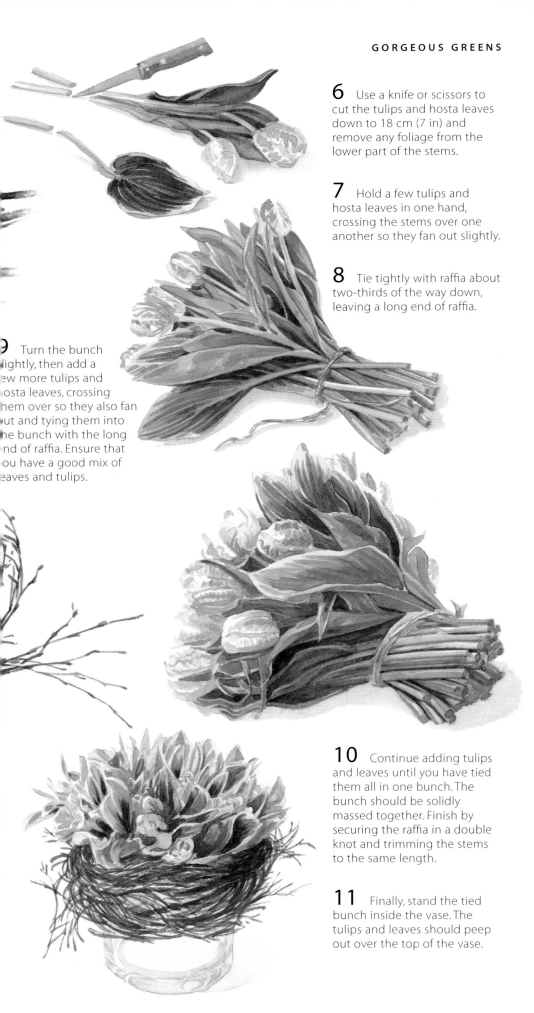

6 Use a knife or scissors to cut the tulips and hosta leaves down to 18 cm (7 in) and remove any foliage from the lower part of the stems.

7 Hold a few tulips and hosta leaves in one hand, crossing the stems over one another so they fan out slightly.

8 Tie tightly with raffia about two-thirds of the way down, leaving a long end of raffia.

9 Turn the bunch slightly, then add a few more tulips and hosta leaves, crossing them over so they also fan out and tying them into the bunch with the long end of raffia. Ensure that you have a good mix of leaves and tulips.

10 Continue adding tulips and leaves until you have tied them all in one bunch. The bunch should be solidly massed together. Finish by securing the raffia in a double knot and trimming the stems to the same length.

11 Finally, stand the tied bunch inside the vase. The tulips and leaves should peep out over the top of the vase.

1 Wrap and tie the wire around the top and centre of the bowl to make an anchor for the birch twigs.

2 Trim the twigs down to 90 cm (36 in) and remove any small branches from the bottom 10 cm (4 in). Tie some wire tightly around the end of one of the trimmed twigs.

3 Position the twig against the side of the bowl, and tie it in to one of the wire circles. Tie it in again at intervals along its length.

4 Repeat with a second birch twig, attaching it to the first and staggering it so the two overlap. Tie the second twig into the anchor wire.

5 Continue tying and wrapping twigs until the top half of the bowl is surrounded with a 'necklace' of twigs. Fill the bowl two-thirds full of water.

limelight roses

This beautiful lime-green rose is one of the latest wonders produced by the rose breeders. It opens just like the old-fashioned cabbage roses that I remember as a child. How decadent to use so many of them in a glass bowl lined with fresh limes. If you can't find lime-green roses, orange ones accompanied by orange slices would look equally stunning. Keep the mood cool and fresh with crisp table linen and a very large glass of chilled white wine.

materials & equipment

glass bowl, 22 cm (9 in) high x 25 cm (10 in) diameter

inner bowl, 20 cm (8 in) high x 20 cm (8 in) diameter

1 block floral foam, 32 x 23 x 18 cm (13 x 9 x 7 in)

30–40 limes

70–80 green roses

floristry knife • floristry scissors

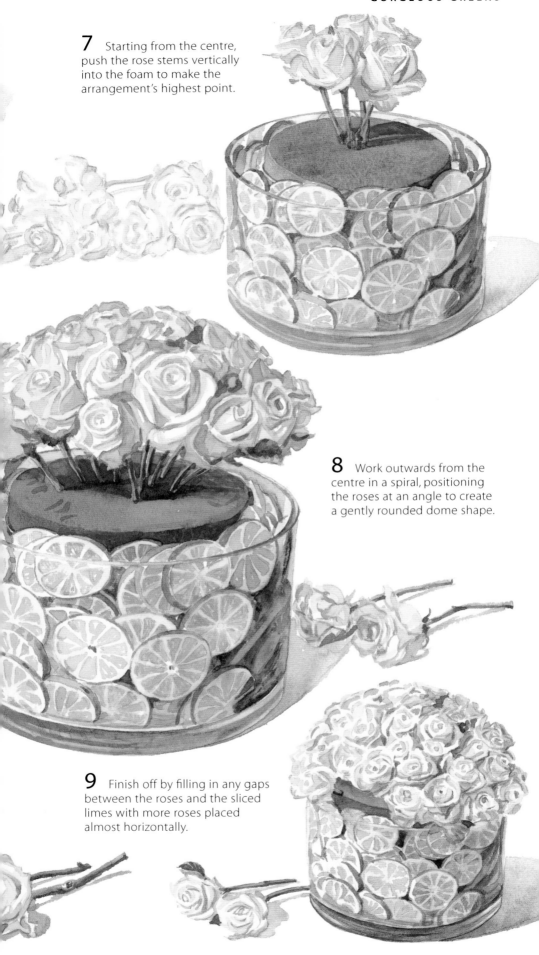

7 Starting from the centre, push the rose stems vertically into the foam to make the arrangement's highest point.

8 Work outwards from the centre in a spiral, positioning the roses at an angle to create a gently rounded dome shape.

9 Finish off by filling in any gaps between the roses and the sliced limes with more roses placed almost horizontally.

1 Place the inner bowl upside down on the block of floral foam and push it down, using the edges of the bowl to cut a circle from the foam.

2 Soak the foam circle plus the offcuts in a bucket of water, then place the soaked offcuts in the bottom of the inner bowl.

3 Place the soaked foam circle on top of the offcuts so the foam comes roughly 5 cm (2 in) above the rim of the bowl. Place the inner bowl inside the outer one.

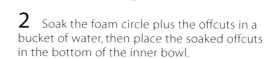

4 Cut the limes into 5 mm (¼ in) slices.

5 Fill the space between the two bowls with the sliced limes.

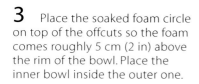

6 Use scissors to cut the stems of the roses down to18 cm (7 in), then remove any thorns and the foliage from the lower part of the stems.

orient express

If you're cooking Chinese, Thai or Japanese, then you'll want your table centre to match your culinary skills. Cover the table with green felt, add square amber-coloured candles, square dishes and chopsticks and place a square dish in the centre filled with exotic flowers and foliage. Position a tiny orchid floret between each pair of chopsticks and your guests can practise their chopstick skills while waiting for dinner to arrive.

materials & equipment

glass dish, 34 x 34 x 5 cm (14 x 14 x 2 in)

1 block floral foam, 32 x 23 x 18 cm (13 x 9 x 7 in)

5 sunflowers

2 fatsia leaves

6 variegated hosta leaves

3 stems bamboo, 30 cm (12 in) long

3 stems papyrus

30 stems crocosmia seed heads

9 cymbidium orchid florets

floristry knife • floristry scissors • florist's tape • medium-gauge stub wires
raffia • wire cutters • reel wire • fine-gauge stub wires

5 Tie the three lengths of bamboo cane together using pieces of raffia.

6 Lay the bundle of bamboo at a slight angle across one side of the foam and pin in place with medium-gauge stub wires bent into hairpin shapes.

7 Cut the stems of papyrus down to 7cm (3 in) and arrange them in the centre of the foam.

8 Use spool wire to wire together three clusters of crocosmia seed heads and space them evenly around the edge of the floral foam.

9 Use fine-gauge stub wires to wire up the orchid florets and push them in the foam to cover any gaps.

1 Soak the floral foam in water then cut it into a 12 x 20 x 10 cm (5 x 8 x 4 in) block. Use florist's tape to attach the soaked floral foam to the glass dish.

2 Remove the petals from the sunflowers.

3 Trim the sunflower stems right down, then bend varying lengths of medium-gauge stub wires into hairpin shapes and use to attach the sunflower centres to one corner of the floral foam.

4 Position the fatsia leaves in the opposite corner, then wire together two bunches of three hosta leaves and push into the foam, either side of the fatsia leaves.

kitchen-garden cabbages

This arrangement in a painted trug is so easy to do and is just perfect for an informal lunch or dinner in the garden. To complete the picture, tie matching napkins with raffia. If you are entertaining on a larger scale and need arrangements for several small tables, use small garden trugs and fill them with mini cabbages.

materials & equipment

garden trug, 55 x 30 x 10 cm (22 x 12 x 4 in)

sage-green oil-based paint

3 blocks floral foam, 32 x 23 x 18 cm (13 x 9 x 7 in)

plastic sheeting, to fit

5 cm (2 in) chicken wire, to cover floral foam

21–30 green ornamental cabbages, in a selection of varieties

paintbrush • floristry scissors • florist's tape • floristry knife

6 Trim the stems of the ornamental cabbages to 20 cm (8 in) and remove any leaves from the lower part of the stems.

7 Starting at the centre of the trug, push the stems of the ornamental cabbages into the foam, arranging them vertically, in clusters of three cabbages of the same variety.

8 Work outwards from the centre, cutting the cabbage stems further if necessary to give a gently domed shape.

9 As you reach the edge of the trug, arrange the cabbages at an angle to ensure that the edge is completely concealed.

98

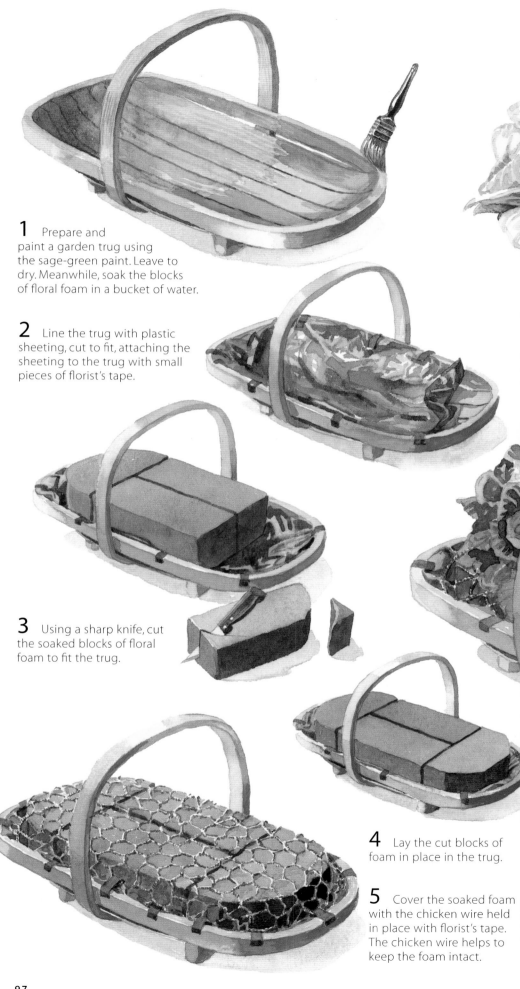

1 Prepare and paint a garden trug using the sage-green paint. Leave to dry. Meanwhile, soak the blocks of floral foam in a bucket of water.

2 Line the trug with plastic sheeting, cut to fit, attaching the sheeting to the trug with small pieces of florist's tape.

3 Using a sharp knife, cut the soaked blocks of floral foam to fit the trug.

4 Lay the cut blocks of foam in place in the trug.

5 Cover the soaked foam with the chicken wire held in place with florist's tape. The chicken wire helps to keep the foam intact.

left Blues and mauves are dreamy finished with a wisp of chiffon and a single anemone.
right Over-the-top plates call for a napkin tied with as much romance as you can muster. Perfect for a good, old-fashioned tea-time with dainty sandwiches and tiny iced sponge cakes.
far right Lively music and informal food are what you need for this bright combination of young-at-heart glassware with wildly coloured table linen.

table settings

While it's not realistic to have dozens of different sets of crockery, cutlery, glassware or table linen, planning table flowers around what you have rather than fighting it reaps its rewards. Well chosen combinations of colours and styles that harmonise and complement each other cannot be bettered. This attention to detail can make or break the show. The results are sure to win you praise.

top The scale's just right. A single stem of grape hyacinths and a chiffon bow make the perfect tie.
above Keep festive flowers unfussy when the tableware is plain, modern and white.
right Contemporary cutlery sparkles against white linen.

table accessories

Enhance the mood, indulge your dreams and make your
arrangements of table flowers burst with extra individuality
and personality. It's easy to do with a drift of candles or
nightlights, a scattering of petals, a fine birchwood skewer
of leaves, petals and tiny vegetables, or tumbling clusters
of richly coloured fruits. These are the extras that allow
you to let your hair down – the details that will make
your table arrangements truly memorable.

Candles add atmosphere to any
occasion and come in a wide
range of colours and styles,
though I prefer simple cream
ones. Best of all are church
candles. They are always good
quality, smokeless, and last forever.
top Tall, multi-wick candles cast
their extra brightness on the table.
above left Nightlights in square
holders reflect a coppery glow.
above right The Orient arrives
with bamboo-shaped candles.
far left The silvery sheen of
frosted glass always looks good.
left White light gleaming on blue
glass is a classic combination.

above Twigs and foliage sprayed with gold and silver paint are more or less *de rigueur* for any Christmas display, but you can be a good deal more subtle about it if you lay a shimmery, silvery gauze chiffon over silver-sprayed holly leaves on a white linen cloth. Gold chiffon with gold-sprayed leaves would work just as well, or try pink, red or rich orange rose petals with a toning gauzy covering.

right Boldly extravagant massed lilac-pink tulips and roses in silver vases really take your breath away. Indulge the extravagance still further with a shower of matching pink rose heads at their feet.

below Skewers of small fruits, vegetables, petals and leaves in bold colours like these can be piled up as a table centrepiece or placed on each guest's side plate.

below right Packed full of clementines, these toning orange wine glasses become an integral part of the table decoration.

a few essentials

Having the correct tools and materials for flower arranging can make all the difference between doing the job quickly and efficiently, and ending up annoyed and frustrated. Similarly, knowing the best way to prepare and maintain beautiful but ephemeral plant material will ensure that it lasts as long as possible. You don't want to find that, after a day or two, all your hard work is ready to be thrown away. Read these tips and be well prepared. It's worth it . . . honest!

essential tools and materials

Sharp floristry scissors are a must for making your flower arrangements. Use them for collecting plant material from the garden and for trimming stems down to size. If you are dealing with thick, woody stems, use floristry secateurs rather than scissors. When you are collecting material from your own garden, take a bucket of water with you so you can put the flowers and foliage in water straightaway and so minimise wilting.

A sharp floristry knife is also useful for cutting stems to length or for stripping them of foliage and thorns. Use one, too, for trimming floral foam.

Floral foam is the basis for many of the arrangements in this book. It was invented in 1954 but was not widely available and affordable until the 1970s. Until then, moss was mostly used. Floral foam is more versatile, though, and holds the flowers more securely, but it must be cleverly concealed. When using it in a porous container, be sure to line the container with plastic sheeting to prevent water seeping out. The foam comes in two versions – green for fresh flowers, and brown for dried. Both can be cut with a sharp knife, and both are available in a variety of ready-made shapes, the most common of which are blocks of differing sizes, and balls. Other ready-made shapes such as hearts, cones or letters of the alphabet can be purchased, as well as plastic-based flat designer boards that can be cut to any shape.

Floral foam for fresh-flower arrangements must be soaked in water before use. To do this, float it in a bucket of water. Once it sinks to the bottom (do not push it) and air bubbles stop rising to the surface, it is ready for use. It can only be soaked once. If you try to soak it a second time, it will disintegrate. Leave the soaked foam to stand to allow any excess water to drain out – you can put it on a cake-cooling rack or a trivet so you can tell when water has stopped leaking – then place it in your chosen container and you are ready to start arranging flowers in it.

To support heavy or hollow stems, use chicken wire. It comes in different gauges for stems of different diameters. Crumple it into a ball and place in the vase. If you are using a glass vase, you will have to disguise the wire with moss.

Wire is essential for supporting many flower and foliage stems, especially soft or thin ones, and is also needed for fruits and vegetables. Choose from stub

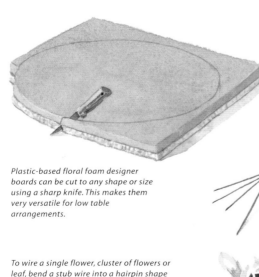

Plastic-based floral foam designer boards can be cut to any shape or size using a sharp knife. This makes them very versatile for low table arrangements.

To wire a single flower, cluster of flowers or leaf, bend a stub wire into a hairpin shape with one leg longer than the other. Hold the bent end next to the stem or stems, then wind the long leg around the stem and the short leg. Use fine-gauge wire for delicate flowers and individual florets, and heavier wire for tougher material.

To wire up a piece of fruit, push several heavy-gauge stub wires right through the bottom third of the fruit, then bring the ends around and twist them together. The heavier the fruit, the more wires you will need.

This arrangement uses many of the essential tools and materials of flower arranging. The porous container is lined with plastic sheeting that has been cut to size and secured using lengths of florist's tape, and the soaked floral foam blocks are also held in place with tape. The ivy garlands are tied to the handles of the container using reel wire.

wires or reel wire. Stub wires come in different thicknesses and lengths. Use the finer ones for delicate flowers and foliage and for wiring individual florets, and the thicker ones for woody stems, vegetables and fruits. You will need reel wire for binding work, for example when making twig 'skirts' or 'necklaces', or for binding lengths of ivy together into garlands and for tying them to vase handles.

Wire cutters are essential for cutting reel wire, stub wires and chicken wire, and you may find pliers useful to bend thick stub wires or chicken wire into shape.

Green florist's tape is another essential. It is waterproof, comes in different widths and is used for securing wet floral foam in a vase or other container, and for making a criss-cross grid over the mouth of a vase. It is also used for attaching wires or wooden sticks to candles (see below).

Plastic sheeting is essential for lining porous containers so water does not leak out and ruin your furnishings. You can cut this to size using ordinary household scissors. By the time you have finished making the arrangement, the plastic will not show.

When making hand-tied bunches, I prefer to bind the flowers with raffia or chunky string. These have the advantage of looking good, which is something to bear in mind in case the bunch is to be placed in a glass vase, but you could just as easily use ordinary string or even a few elastic bands.

Topiary trees make lovely arrangements but the stems have to be well-supported. Use quick-drying cement in an inner container which is then placed in an outer

To prevent accidents, candles must be firmly fixed in the floral foam. Use special candle holders, or simply attach matchsticks or wires around the base of the candle, leaving the ends protruding.

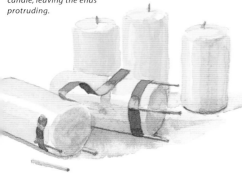

display pot. The reason for this is that the cement sometimes cracks the pot as it dries. Once the arrangement has died, you can always keep the stick in its pot to make another display.

Other miscellaneous items you will need are household scissors for trimming the plastic sheeting and for cutting ribbon trims, ordinary dressmaking pins or pins with decorative heads for attaching leaves to tablecloths or to the edge of foam bases, and some medium-sized paintbrushes for painting containers to harmonize with the flowers.

anchoring candles

There are special holders available from florists for anchoring standard-size candles in floral foam, but these are not really necessary as you can easily make supports using wire or wooden sticks – medium-gauge wire, cocktail sticks or matchsticks are ideal for small and medium-sized candles; you will need heavy-gauge wire or wooden skewers for fatter candles. For wire supports, cut the wire into lengths of between 10 and 20 cm (4-8 in), depending on the diameter of the candle, and bend them into U-shapes. Hold the bent wires in position against the base of the candle so the wires protrude, and tape them in place with florist's tape. If you are using wooden sticks, simply trim them to length and tape them round the base of the candle in the same way. The candles can now be positioned securely in the floral foam, using the protruding wire or wood inserted in the foam.

To group several candles, tape their bases together with florist's tape and incorporate wire or wooden supports as you would for one candle.

conditioning plant material

To ensure a long life for your cut flowers – especially those that are to be arranged in floral foam – you must start with good-quality material. If economy is a factor, choose flowers that are in season. Out-of-season flowers and foliage will always be more expensive. Buy from a reputable supplier and choose blooms with firm petals. Any buds should be showing some colour or they will not develop. Make sure the florist wraps the flowers properly, and if they are to be out of water for several hours, ask for the stem ends to be covered with damp paper.

When you get the flowers home, trim their stems by at least 2.5 cm (1 in), cutting at an angle to expose the maximum surface area, and give them a deep drink of lukewarm water – preferably containing flower food – for several hours. This will firm up the stems and is especially important for flowers that are to be arranged in foam, since over the next few days, their supply of water will be limited.

Flowers such as euphorbias exude a milky liquid when cut, so for their first deep drink, you should separate them from other flowers.

The narcissus family also poses problems. They exude 'daffodil slime' that is harmful to other flowers. If you want them in mixed arrangements, first put them in a bucket of water on their own for twelve hours and do not re-cut their stems afterwards. Alternatively, you can use a special narcissus flower food that overcomes this problem.

Before you arrange the plant material, re-trim the stems to the desired length. Again, cut them at an angle and never crush or pierce them, or use blunt knives and scissors. This destroys their water-carrying vessels, which inhibits water uptake and so promotes the growth of bacteria. It also causes undue stress which shortens the flowers' life. Remove any foliage that will be under water, otherwise this will rot, producing bacteria that will shorten the life of the flowers in the vase. Specimens such as carnations, which have nodules on the stems, should be cut just above, not below, a nodule.

As a final tip, remove any tightly closed buds from the top of the stems. These will not open until the lower blooms have faded and died. If you do not remove them, they will greedily take up all the water and deprive the other blooms.

Most flowers are now ready to be arranged but one or two species will last longer if specially treated. Roses, especially hothouse-grown ones, have weak stems and the heads often droop. To minimise this, wrap their heads in paper to protect them and plunge the stems into boiling water for a few minutes.

Tulips are another example. These continue growing after they are cut, and as they grow, they twist and turn towards the light. To prevent this, or if you want to straighten them after they have been in an arrangement for a few days, re-trim the stems, wrap in stiff paper with the paper extending above the flowers but not covering the lower third of the stems, and put in lukewarm water, deep enough to submerge the exposed stems. Leave in a cool place for a couple of hours and they will straighten.

Hollow-stemmed flowers, such as amaryllis and hyacinths, will last longer if you fill their stems with water and then plug them with cotton wool, while poppies last better if their stems are singed in a flame.

arranging tips
Always make sure that the container you use is scrupulously clean. Soak it in a dilute solution of bleach to kill any bacteria, as bacteria will shorten the life of your cut flowers.

While you are working, protect your surfaces with plastic sheeting, and keep the cut flowers and foliage in water all the time, to minimise wilting.

Arrange your flowers in lukewarm water. This contains less oxygen than cold, so helps prevent the air bubbles that will block the flowers' water uptake. But daffodils and tulips prefer cold water.

Unless you are arranging tulips, always add cut-flower food to the water. This feeds the flowers and foliage, keeps bacteria at bay, encourages buds to open and lengthens the life of your flowers.

Wherever possible, for arrangements in floral foam, avoid hollow-stemmed and soft-stemmed material.

Do not put flowers near ripening fruit. The fruit releases ethylene gas which prematurely ages the flowers. For this reason, regard arrangements that combine flowers and fruit as being more short-term than those that consist only of flowers.

Lily pollen stains clothes and walls, so pinch out the stamens before arranging lilies.

For better visual impact, group your flowers and foliage in clusters, as in the projects in this book.

maintenance
If flowers and foliage have been well conditioned, an arrangement should last up to a week. Those in foam have a slightly shorter life. To extend the life of any arrangement as much as possible, keep it away from direct heat, sunlight and draughts, and top up the water regularly, adding more flower food from time to time (except in the case of tulips). For arrangements in foam, you should check daily if the foam is still moist, and only add water when it starts to dry out.

Remove dead flower heads and foliage. These look unsightly and, like ripening fruit, give off ethylene which will shorten the life of the arrangement.

To revive flowers that are wilting, you can try running cool water over the stems and spraying the petals with water from a plant mister. Wilting violets can be revived by immersing the flower heads completely in a vase of water for about an hour.

plant directory

Anemone *(Anemone coronaria)*
pp. 30, 34, 70, 74
There are many varieties available, but the best commercially grown ones come from Italy. Change their water regularly and keep them cool.

Arum lily *(Zantedeschia aethiopica)*
p. 52
This most elegant of flowers works well as a single stem or *en masse* with no other flowers. It is long lasting.

Bamboo *(Bambusa vulgaris) p. 92*
Available in many lengths and diameters, it is very long lasting, needing no water or special care. It will slowly lose its green colour.

Birch *(Betula) pp. 60, 84*
Cut birch will last almost forever. Keep it in a small amount of clean water.

Cabbage *(Brassica oleracea*
var. capitata) p. 96
Not to be eaten! Add a tiny drop of household bleach to the water and change the water and trim the stems regularly or the water will smell.

Crocosmia *(Crocosmia) p.92*
The sprays of red or orange flowers produce attractive seed heads that will slowly dry out. They are long lasting.

Cymbidium orchid *(Cymbidium) p. 92*
These exotic flowers are expensive but long lasting, so worth the money.

Fatsia *(Fatsia) p. 92*
These leaves look great lining vases or in contemporary arrangements.

Gloriosa superba *(Gloriosa superba)*
p. 52
These showy, exotic-looking blooms look stunning both in mixed arrangements or on their own. Remove most of their leaves before arranging as these have a tendency to die quickly.

Grape hyacinth *(Muscari) p. 34*
These fragile spring flowers come in white and shades of blue. They are easily grown in the garden.

Hosta *(Hosta) pp. 84, 92*
Hosta leaves come in a wide range of colours and shapes, from broad, heavily ribbed glaucous blue, to narrow, pointed and green variegated with cream or off-white. They are stunning for contemporary arrangements but their disadvantage is their short stems, so wiring is usually necessary.

Hydrangea *(Hydrangea) pp. 16, 42, 70*
Available in white, cream, bright blue or lime green, these look wonderful in garden or vase. Cut the stem at an angle and plunge into boiling water to seal. They are quite temperamental and dislike extremes of heat or cold.

Hypericum *(Hypericum) p. 56*
This has glorious reddish-brown berries and incredibly long-lasting foliage. It looks great with berried ivy.

Ivy *(Hedera) pp. 12, 16, 20, 24, 30, 34, 38, 42, 52, 56, 60, 70, 74, 78*
A very long-lasting glossy foliage with leaves ranging from large and dark green (which can be used singly) to small and variegated. Long, trailing stems of ivy can give a lift to an arrangement while its black winter berries add to its usefulness.

Lichen-covered larch *(Larix) p. 70*
These delightfully textured twigs can be used to add a wintry feel to an arrangement. They last for ages, but you should change the water regularly.

Lisianthus *(Eustoma grandiflorum)*
p. 34
Delicate-looking but long lasting, these need to be conditioned in cold water.

Moss *p. 74*
In a variety of colours and textures, this very versatile ingredient can be used to fill in gaps or to wrap round bowls and vases. Spray with water to keep it fresh.

Oak *(Quercus) p. 48*
Oak has many different leaf shapes, all of which look good in arrangements. Cut the branches when the leaves are just turning golden-brown, then they will remain attractive for the longest possible time. Huge branches look great arranged in a large vase, or else just use the leaves on their own, scattered on the tabletop.

Papyrus *(Cyperus papyrus) p. 92*
This textural foliage is very elegant and sculptural and will last well if you trim the stems regularly.

Poppy *(Papaver) p. 56*
Very delicate, these flowers need love and tenderness. Singe the ends of the cut stems to seal them.

Rose *(Rosa) pp. 12, 24, 34, 38, 52, 56, 66, 70, 78, 88*
The queen of flowers and a great choice for any occasion. Spray roses are a new development and are useful where a lighter look is required. Cut the stems at an angle under running water and change the water in the vase frequently. Roses like to be kept away from direct light and heat.

Rosemary *(Rosmarinus) pp. 24, 70*
Traditionally symbolic of remembrance, rosemary has a most wonderful smell and is long lasting. Everyone should grow it, either in the garden or in a pot.

Snowberry *(Symphoricarpos) p. 12*
This lovely shrub produces attractive luscious white and pinkish-white berries that are especially useful for late autumn and winter arrangements.

Spiraea *(Spiraea) p. 70*
This versatile, long-lasting foliage has wonderful deep red florets that look good in any red arrangement.

Sunflower *(Helianthus annuus)*
pp. 60, 92
Remove most of the leaves before arranging as these die quickly. If the heads droop, re-cut the stems and plunge them in boiling water for 60 seconds – a trick that also works for roses and gerberas.

Tulip *(Tulipa) pp. 20, 38, 48, 56, 70, 84*
Providing a most wonderful choice and available for an increasingly long season, tulips, like all flowers from bulbs, will continue to grow after they have been cut and put in water, and this makes them doubly interesting as cut flowers. Trim them regularly and keep away from light as they have a tendency to grow towards it, giving arrangements a lopsided look.

suppliers

Flowers & foliage

John Austin Co. Ltd
Stand M5 Flower Market
New Covent Garden Market
London SW8 5NB
The best quality and selection of
fresh flowers, with flowers
imported from Holland and Italy.

Baker & Duguid
251–252 Flower Market
New Covent Garden Market
London SW8 5NA

Flowers and Plants Association
Covent House
New Covent Garden Market
London SW8 5NX
Organization that can be
contacted for advice and tips on
flower care.

Derek Hardcastle Ltd
Stand M4 Flower Market
New Covent Garden Market
London SW8 5NA

E. Pollard & Sons
Flower Market
P. O. Box 356
New Covent Garden Market
London SW8 5EF

Ronald Porter & Sons
P28–31 Flower Market
New Covent Garden Market
London SW8 5HH
Best quality foliage.

J. Ray Wholesale
373 Flower Market
New Covent Garden Market
London SW8 5NB

Sundries

B & Q
Branches nationwide; for nearest
branch, phone 0181 466 4166
Stocks a good selection of plants,
tools and florist's sundries.

Cocuerel's Sundries
313–314 Flower Market
New Covent Garden Market
London SW8 5NF
All florist's sundries.

Costerwise Ltd
Studio A
Royalty Studios
105-109 Lancaster Road
London W11 1QF
Great suppliers of brown paper.

Donover Bros. Ltd
165 Childers Street
Deptford SE8
All sundries.

Homebase
Branches nationwide; for nearest
branch, phone 0645 801 800
Stocks a good selection of plants,
tools and florist's sundries.

Smithers-Oasis UK Ltd
Crowther Road
Crowther Industrial Estate
Washington
Tyne & Wear
BG7 6HA
Manufacturers of accessories for
flower arranging and a range of
floral foam products, including
bricks and wreath frames, in a vast
range of sizes and shapes.

Ribbons

J. T. Morgan
28 Chepstow Corner
Chepstow Place
London W2 4XA

V. V. Rouleaux
54 Sloane Square
London SW1
Wonderful range of ribbons in all
widths and textures, including
wire-edged ribbon.

Urns, vases, etc

Bowles & Linares
820A Harrow Road
London NW10 5QJ

Capital Garden Products
Gibbs Road Barn
Pashley Road
Ticehurst
East Sussex TN5 7HE

Carden & Cunetti
Westbourne Park Road
London W11

Clifton Nurseries
5A Clifton Villas
London W9 2PH

L. S. A
Unit E
The Dolphine Estate
Windmill Road
Sunbury on Thames
Middlesex TW16 7HE

Marston & Langiner
192 Mozart Terrace
Ebury Street
London SW1 8UP

Candles

Aero
96 Westbourne Grove
London W2 5RX

Carden Cunietti
83 Westbourne Park Road
London W2

Habitat
196 Tottenham Court Road
London W1P 9LD

Heal's
196 Tottenham Court Road
London W1P 9LD

Price's Candles
110 York Road
Battersea
London SW11 3RO

Space
Westbourne Grove
London W11

credits

**Asprey & Garrard, 167 New Bond Street, London W1
Tel: 0171 493 6767**
p. 46 champagne flute; p. 47 *left* gold plates,
right gold plates; p. 55 gold plates.

**Maryse Boxer at Joseph, 26 Sloane Street, London SW1
Tel: 0171 245 9493**
p. 15 patterned glasses with gold rim.

**Carden Cunietti, 83 Westbourne Park Road, London W2
Tel: 0171 229 8559**
p. 83 *left* oriental-style bamboo candles; p. 102
above right oriental-style bamboo candles.

**The Conran Shop, Michelin House, 81 Fulham Road,
London SW3 Tel: 0171 589 7401**
p. 11 *left* white plates, *below* wooden bowl,
right tablecloth; p. 15 white plates; pp. 16-19 fabric cloth;
pp. 20-23 napkin; p. 29 *right* silver vase, *below* blue glass
bottles; pp. 38-41 metal ridged vase; pp. 42-45 patterned
blue glasses; p. 46 gold candles; pp. 74-77 glasses; p. 82
above right plates and chopsticks; p. 83 *left* tea bowls; pp.
92-95 large square glass dish; p. 96 cloth and napkins; p.
101 *far right* decorative glassware; p. 103 *right* silver vases.

**Designers Guild, 267-271 and 275-277 Kings Road,
London SW3 5EN Tel: 0171 351 5775**
pp. 88-91 napkins and place mats; p101
far right tablecloth and napkins.

**General Trading Company, 144 Sloane Street, London
SW1 Tel: 0171 730 0411**
pp. 24-27 horn beakers; p. 47 *above left* tea glasses,
right flower-patterned glasses.

**Thomas Goode, 19 South Audley Street, London W1
Tel: 0171 499 2823**
p. 29 *far right* glass vases p. 47 *left* gold napkin ring;
p. 66-69 candelabra; p. 73 garnet-coloured wine glasses;
p. 81 teacups and saucers and glass cake stand;
p. 101 *right* tea plate.

**Interiors bis, 60 Sloane Street, London SW3
Tel: 0171 838 1104**
p. 15 white pot; p. 16 white plates.

**John Lewis, Oxford Street, London W1
Tel: 0171 629 7711**
p. 28 chiffon cloth; p. 81 chiffon cloth.

**Marston & Langinger, 192 Ebury Street, London SW1
Tel: 0171 824 8818**
pp. 96-99 wooden garden trug.

**Mulberry, 219 Kings Road, London SW3
Tel: 0171 352 1871**
p. 55 gold gilt-rim glass.

**Oggetti, 143 Fulham Road, London SW3
Tel: 0171 584 9808**
p. 101 *right* contemporary cutlery; p. 103 *above* silver
cutlery and white plates.

**The Pier, 200 Tottenham Court Road, London W1
Tel: 0171 814 5020**
pp. 56-59 glass goblets; pp. 74-77 square candles;
p. 103 *below right* orange wine glasses.

**V. V. Rouleaux, 54 Sloane Square, London SW1
Tel: 0171 730 3125**
p. 11 *left* ribbon; pp. 20-23 ribbon; pp. 34-37 ribbon;
pp. 42-45 ribbon; pp. 78-81 ribbon; p. 101 *right* ribbon;
p. 101 *top* chiffon ribbon for bow.

**Space, 214 Westbourne Grove, London W11
Tel: 0171 229 6533**
p. 10 *below* square candles; p. 11 *right* white rectangular
ceramic vases pp. 24-27 square candles; p. 102 *above left*
candles in square holders.

**Wild at Heart Ltd., Turquoise Island, 22 Westbourne
Grove, London W11 2RJ Tel: 0171 229 1174**
p. 10 *left* candles and nightlight glasses, *below* stone
bowl; pp. 16-19 urn and candles; pp. 20-23 nightlight
glasses and square vases; pp. 24-27 concrete bowl;
p. 29 *right* tall stem glass vases; pp. 30-31 urn;
pp. 34-37 candles; pp. 42-45 candles; p. 46 glass bowl on
a stem; p. 47 *far left* galvanized vases; pp. 48-51 glass
bowls; pp. 52-55 galvanized trough; pp. 56-59 wire urn;
pp. 56-59 nightlight glasses; pp. 60-63 glass vase;
p. 64 *right* goldfish bowl; p. 64 *left* rectangular glass vase;
p. 65 *left* clear glass vase; p. 65 *below* galvanized
bucket; pp. 70-73 two-tier candelabra and candles;
pp. 74-77 glass tank vases; pp. 78-81 glass bowl with a
stem; p. 82 *above left* stemmed glass bowl; p. 82 *left* large
cylindrical glass vase; p. 83 *right* and *below* glass vase;
pp. 84-87 glass bowl; pp. 88-91 glass bowl; p. 102 *top*
multi-wick candles; p. 102 *left* and *far left* blue glass
nightlight glasses and frosted glass nightlight glasses;
p. 105 urn.

p. 15 wine goblets; pp. 42-45 napkins; p. 81 napkins;
p. 100 napkins: stylist's own.

acknowledgements

It has been a wonderful experience to produce this book, and a great opportunity to work with Simon Brown and Lucy Berridge.

It was fun, rewarding and a huge, huge, huge pleasure. It's always a treat to work with such professional people who have so much love for their work. I only hope they feel the same!

Of course I wouldn't have been able to produce this book without the help of others. My most special thanks and love must go to Jo Shipp, who has worked with Wild At Heart since she left college. We have grown together in our passion for flowers. She is inspired and truly inspirational. Marisa Mauri and Charlotte Seddon are Wild at Heart. Without them I wouldn't be doing what I do, Wild At Heart wouldn't be Wild At Heart, and I will never be able to thank them enough.

Anna Kearney runs my life and my office – she deserves a medal. What would I do without her? I also want to thank Victoria Brotherson for always being there from the very beginning, and special, special thanks must go, too, to Kat, Kate, Sarah, Coleen and Michelle. And a special thank you to everyone at New Covent Garden Flower Market, especially Dennis, Chris and Eric at John Austin & Co. Ltd., to Barry at Ronald Porter and to Brian at Derek Hardcastle. Without you there would be no flowers or foliage!

And finally, Sally Powell and Hilary Mandleberg deserve an enormous thank you for all their help, support and patience. Sorry!

The publishers would like to thank Belinda Battle, Phillip Billingham and Heidi Wish, Siobhan Squire and Gavin Lynsey, and Lulu Guinness for allowing us to photograph in their homes. With thanks also to Mission.